Worldwatch Paper 37

Women, Men, and The Division of Labor

Kathleen Newland

May 1980

THE WORLDWATCH PAPER SERIES

(continued on inside back cover)

Worldwatch Institute is an independent, non-profit research organization created to analyze and to focus attention on global problems. Directed by Lester R. Brown, Worldwatch is funded by private foundations, United Nations organizations, and governmental agencies. Worldwatch papers are written for a worldwide audience of decision makers, scholars, and the general public.

Women, Men, and The Division of Labor

Kathleen Newland

Worldwatch Paper 37

May 1980

Table of Contents

The sexual division of labor is probably the oldest one in human history. The division of labor into paid and unpaid work is a more recent invention, but it has often coincided with boundaries drawn according to sex. Thus paid employment is dominated by men while women's work is concentrated in the unpaid, household sector. The division is by no means a pure one, and never has been. But it has been widespread, and, perhaps more significantly, it has been widely held up as a social ideal. The family with a breadwinning father and a mother who stays at home to run the household and raise the children has been seen as a "normal" family, particularly for the middle classes and those who aspire to middle-class status.

Both as a fact and as an ideal, however, the division that places most men in paid labor and most women in unpaid labor is breaking down. Nearly half the world's adult women are in the labor force—a category that excludes women who do only unpaid work at home. The view, never very accurate, that employment outside the household is a secondary role for women is therefore increasingly at odds with the facts. Awareness of the major role that women play in the labor market is slowly beginning to make its way into the arena of public policy. National and international conferences, reports, resolutions, and programs have addressed themselves to the new realities of women's employment.

Amid this furor of activity, one issue remains so untouched that one can easily conclude that it represents the eye of the storm: the sharing of unpaid, household labor between women and men receives only a fraction of the attention given to equality in formal employment. If women are to take full advantage of newly won access to the formal labor market, men must increase their share of the essential work that goes on outside of it. Otherwise, equal opportunity for women will turn out to be a recipe for overwork.

6 British sociologists Michael Young and Peter Willmott have described the interaction between men's work and women's work in terms of a historical progression. In the first phase, men and women both work to support the household in subsistence production. Men's and women's ways of supporting the family diverge in the second phase, with the development of a split between women's unpaid work in the household and men's "breadwinning." In the third phase, women increasingly share the breadwinning role with men, but retain most of the responsibility for the home. The as-yet-unrealized ideal of the fourth phase is a "symmetrical family," as Young and Willmott describe it, in which both the financial support and the physical maintenance of the family are equally shared between men and women.[1]

History never proceeds so neatly through well-defined stages. But abstractions are helpful in thinking about the real changes that are taking place in the way work is divided between women and men. In most societies today the division resembles the second phase described by Young and Willmott more closely than it does the first stage, and in many countries a substantial number of people have made the transition to the third phase. The symmetrical family, however, remains a rarity. Each transition amounts to a major, historic shift in the organization of human labors, with far-reaching consequences for the economy and society.

The industrial revolution ushered in one set of profound changes in the organization of work. Productivity increased enormously, as machines and fossil fuels multiplied human efforts. Production was segmented, and labor became increasingly specialized. The household and the workplace came to be seen as two separate spheres, each with its own distinct functions. The responsibilities of the household were firmly identified as women's work, and women with family responsibilities did not work for pay unless they were compelled to. They depended on men for money and men depended on them for the daily maintenance of the family.

From an economic point of view, this allocation of responsibility seemed efficient, akin to the specialization of labor that so greatly

"As more women have
become involved in paid work,
they have had less time to
devote to unpaid labor
in the household."

increased productivity in the early factories. The division was power-
fully reinforced by stereotyped notions of a woman's nature, which
supposedly equipped her with an instinctive talent for domestic work
and too much delicacy for the rough-and-tumble marketplace. Wom-
en who worked outside the home were seen as either unfortunate
or deliberately perverse.

Even as this view of women's place was institutionalized in the industrial West and exported to much of the rest of the world during the
colonial era, its disadvantages for women became evident: little direct
control over productive resources, limited roles in decision-making,
and great vulnerability to economic adversity.

To overcome the disadvantages of dependent status, and to enjoy the
benefits of economic independence, women in ever-greater numbers
are turning to independent wage-earning. Their growing commitment
to the labor force has led to demands for equal opportunity, equal
wages, and equal treatment in paid employment. In general, governments have responded to or even initiated action on these demands,
though enforcement lags far behind the stated principles. As more
women have become involved in paid work, they have had less time
to devote to unpaid labor in the household—but changes in the division of labor at home have been slow to arrive. The resulting imbalance between men's and women's work loads is at last being
recognized as a social as well as an individual problem.

What the GNP Leaves Out

One major difficulty in evaluating the overall division of labor between women and men stems from the accounting methods used to
keep track of economic activity, which overlook many of the tasks
that women do. When calculating the gross national product (GNP)
of a country, statisticians have to decide how they will define what is
known as the "production boundary." Only those activities they include within the boundary are assigned an economic value and
added to the sum of goods and services produced in the economy.

8 Activities that lie outside the production boundary are left out of the GNP. From there, it is a short step to leaving them out of policy considerations altogether—and such has been the fate of much of women's work.

Measuring the value of goods and services that are never exchanged for money is, obviously, a tricky business. National accounts routinely include some nonmonetary (sometimes called subsistence or nonmarket) items in the GNP. These are goods and services that are used directly by the producers and the members of their households. Most industrial countries include in their accounts only two such items: food produced and consumed on farms and the implied rent that owner-occupiers of dwellings "pay" to themselves. Most developing countries consider a somewhat wider variety of activities in their calculations, taking in such things as firewood gathering, hunting, owner-built housing, home food-processing, or handicrafts. Subsistence agriculture (including livestock production) is counted in almost all countries, but inclusion of the other goods and services that people provide for their own households is much more sporadic. Of 70 developing countries surveyed by the Organisation for Economic Cooperation and Development (OECD) in 1973, for example, only six counted the value of carrying water to its point of use in their GNPs. And only two countries assigned any economic value to housewives' services.[2]

The revised system used by the United Nations to calculate national accounts suggests that one of the main criteria for including an activity in the GNP should be whether it contributes to the well-being of all groups of the population. Another authority recommends that accountants "consider each economic activity as a function of its drain on the community's total scarce resources or of its contribution to the community's total needs."[3]

No one would deny that the provision of water is essential to the welfare—indeed, the survival—of a population or that it is a major drain on the time and energy of those who must carry it where piped water is lacking. But to date the economic valuation of a service depends as much on who does it as on what gets done. In certain regions of Kenya, for example, water carrying is explicitly excluded from national accounting because it is done by women, yet if the same work in the same area was done by men, it would be assigned an economic value.[4]

Designers of national accounting systems frankly admit that another important criterion for counting an activity is the feasibility of measuring its value. Value is measured by price: the price of goods in the marketplace or the price of labor to perform a service, that is, wages. For people who work without pay, economists use the concept of "opportunity cost" to assign to their labors a value equal to the amount those workers presumably could earn if they worked for pay. But national accounts rarely assign an opportunity cost to women's unpaid labor, especially the portion of their effort that goes into providing services for their own households. The production boundary that economists set up almost never encompasses child care, meal preparation, cleaning, crop storage, home care of the sick, and so on. Even heavy work performed by women, such as food processing, wood gathering, and water carrying, is often overlooked. As a result, many hardworking women are classified as "not economically active."

Unpaid labor is not the only kind of work that national income accounts record poorly, if at all. Millions of people, particularly in the Third World, earn money in the informal labor market, at occupations such as petty trading and sales, food preparation, beer brewing, small-scale construction, and such personal services as sewing or barbering. Again, more women than men are involved in this kind of work, much of which is irregular, unskilled, highly competitive, low-profit, and invisible to the eyes of national-income assessors. The modern industrial sector in most poor countries is small. As labor markets become more crowded, women's access to jobs in the formal labor market tends to deteriorate. They get pushed into the informal sector, where earnings and mobility are low but access is easy and requires little capital. As they enter the informal sector, they often disappear from national statistics.

10 The decision about what kind of work to include when calculating national income is an important one. National accounts play a major role in guiding economic policy. They are used to monitor rates and patterns of growth, to set priorities in policymaking, to compare income or production over time or between countries, and to measure the success of particular policies as they are implemented. The GNP is also used, however informally and however inadvisably, as a measure of national welfare. The United Nations uses per capita GNP, for example, to identify nations that most urgently need economic assistance. Almost all governments regard an increase in the GNP as evidence that the well-being of the citizens is improving.

Some of the pitfalls of using GNP as a measure of welfare are well known: increases in cigarette sales and in operations for lung cancer, for example, will produce a rise in GNP, although they signal a deterioration in people's health. And, as described, national accounts especially and consistently overlook and undervalue work done by women, whether in the subsistence sector, the informal labor market, or the household. The consequences of not taking account of the economic value of women's work are serious, both for individual women and for society as a whole. Women who are regarded as "not economically active" have a weak claim on public resources. As in the past, little attention is likely to be given to raising their productivity, relieving their drudgery, or improving their economic security.

Women farmers who work unpaid on family farms, for example, are rarely contacted by agricultural extension agents, even though women are responsible for most of the field work in the developing world. In Zaire, women grow 80 percent of the subsistence crops, yet the agricultural extension programs serve only male farmers. In Upper Volta, where men and women participate equally in agricultural work, there was not a single woman among a staff of over 1,600 agricultural extension agents, technical agricultural agents, and veterinary assistants in the mid-seventies. The result of this neglect was summed up in a report for the International Labour Office (ILO): "In many cases the effect of male-oriented agricultural extension work has been to increase the burden of the women's work. . . .

Moreover, the exclusion of the women from participation in innovations in agricultural methods has slowed down food production and in many cases been a major factor in the failure of projects."[5]

Because of the vital elements of economic life that national accounts often leave out, great skepticism should be attached to the use of GNP as a measure of well-being. The omissions also justify some doubt about the reliability of the GNP as an indicator of economic progress, especially in a country where the patterns of work are shifting rapidly—as they are in most countries today. If more and more women choose or are forced to seek paid employment, the kind and amount of unpaid labor they do is likely to change. National accounts as currently figured give us few tools with which to assess the impact of that change.

Paid Labor: A Man's World No Longer

Women have entered the formal labor force in unprecedented numbers during the past three decades. According to the International Labour Office, the number of women counted as "economically active" rose from 344 million to 576 million between 1950 and 1975. In proportional terms, women made up 35 percent of the global labor force in 1975, up from 31 percent of 1950. Since 1975, the ILO reports, the general upward trend has become even more pronounced —and the agency emphasizes that its figures on working women should be taken as "extremely conservative estimates."[6]

The trend toward greater participation in the labor force on the part of women is most advanced in the Western industrial states and the communist countries in Eastern Europe and East Asia. (See Table 1.) In most of these countries half or more of all adult women are "economically active," most of them working in paid jobs outside the home. In the West, male participation rates have declined slightly, because men have been staying in school longer and retiring at earlier ages. In the United States, for example, as the proportion of women who were employed rose from 34 to 52 percent between

Table 1: Labor Force Participation of Women Since World War II, Selected Countries

Country	Year	Proportion of Adult Women in Labor Force	Year	Proportion of Adult Women in Labor Force
		(percent)		(percent)
Canada	1950	23	1978	48
China	1950	24-40	1975	53
Czechoslovakia	1963	39	1979	70
France	1954	38	1973	48
Hungary	1960	32	1977	82
Japan	1955	57	1978	47
Sweden	1950	34	1976	69
United States	1950	34	1979	51
USSR	1959	49	1978	68

Source: Compiled by the author from ILO, OECD, and government sources.

International Labor Office Organization for Econ Co

1950 and 1980, men's work rate fell from 87 to 77 percent.[7] In other words, the size of the gap between the sexes was more than cut in half—from 53 to 25 percentage points—in 30 years.

In developing countries (except for the Asian communist nations mentioned), the record of women's employment is much more diverse and considerably more difficult to document. Part of the difficulty lies with the unreliability of employment statistics. The extent to which women's work is overlooked in national income accounts was discussed earlier; similarly, labor force statistics tend to overlook many women workers. It is especially difficult to keep accurate tallies of self-employed workers, nonsalaried workers, and unpaid family workers—and in all three of these categories Third World women abound. For example, in Botswana, Nepal, and Tanzania, more than 80 percent of the female labor force is self-employed. Less than 2 percent of the working women in Sierra Leone are salaried employees. And in Gabon and Turkey, eight out of ten work unpaid in family enterprises.[8] Comparisons over time or between countries are not very reliable guides to real changes in the patterns of women's work, because the methods of counting keep changing.

Subject to these limitations, it is possible to identify some trends in the number of women working for pay in groups of Third World countries. Employment opportunities for women have expanded greatly in several Asian and a few Latin American countries as transnational corporations and domestic, export-oriented industries have established labor-intensive manufacturing plants that depend on low-paid female labor. In countries such as Hong Kong, Malaysia, Singapore, and South Korea, the development of the textile, clothing, and electronics industries has produced a rapid expansion in female employment, though the quality of the jobs offered to women is in general desperately low.[9]

In most of Latin America, by contrast, the development of industry has been capital-intensive, limiting the number of jobs available in the modern sector. Intense competition for these few jobs combined with a general climate of sex discrimination in employment has meant that most of the available jobs go to men. Agricultural development in the region has also been capital-intensive. As a result, in much of the region women's involvement in the formal labor force has stagnated or even declined. In Latin America as a whole the crude participation rate of women rose by less than 2 percent between 1950 and 1975. Fourteen percent of the total female population was in the labor force at the end of the period, compared to 12.1 percent at the beginning. In Chile, Ecuador, and Peru, the proportion of women who are in the paid work force actually dropped in the fifties and sixties; in Peru's case it fell from 28 percent in 1950 to only 12 percent in 1970.[10]

In Africa, South Asia, and most of Latin America, female employment hinges on two conflicting pressures. On the one hand, failure of job creation to keep pace with the growth of the labor force produces heightened competition for formal employment, in which women typically lose out to men unless they are much cheaper to hire. On the other hand, ever-increasing numbers of women are compelled to work for pay. The escape valve for this irreconcilable conflict is, increasingly, self-generated employment in the informal sector, particularly in occupations such as street vending or domestic services. Between 1950 and 1970, employment in services absorbed fully 85 percent of the increase in the female labor force in Latin America.[11]

In much of the Third World, the informal sector has come to rival or surpass formal employment as a source of jobs for both men and women. It is the fastest-growing segment of the economy in many African cities, involving 50 to 60 percent of the labor force. A recent report from the U.N. Secretary-General's office characterized the informal service sector as a sort of halfway house between employment and unemployment—a vast reservoir of underemployed labor awaiting economic opportunity.[12] Unfortunately, women are more likely than men to become permanent inhabitants of this halfway house.

Even in those countries where women's participation in formal employment has increased markedly, the range of employment opportunity has remained surprisingly narrow. Women workers in rich and poor countries alike are subject to occupational segregation, which fragments the labor market into stereotypically masculine and feminine jobs. In the nonagricultural labor force, women's work often follows the lines of their traditional household occupations. In the industrial sector, they work in factories producing textiles, garments, footwear, processed food, toys, and so forth. In the service sector, they are concentrated in child care, elementary-school teaching, laundry work, hairdressing, nursing, food service, retail sales, and domestic service. Some jobs that have evolved too recently to acquire a traditional domestic connotation have also become "feminized," such as microelectronic assembly and, in some countries, clerical work.

Occupational segregation operates at the professional level also, usually in a way that severely limits the number of women in high-paying, prestigious, powerful jobs. In virtually any profession—be it business management, politics, or academia—the number of women

"One important element forcing
women into the work force
is the disintegration of families
as a result of
deepening poverty."

dwindles near the top of the hierarchy. In most countries the over-whelming majority of female professionals are teachers or nurses. **15** But there has been some diversification of professional opportuni-ties for women in recent years, especially in the fields of law and medicine. In the United States, for example, nearly one-third of all law students in 1980 are female, compared with only 4 percent in 1965. In Sri Lanka, the proportion of women among newly graduated doctors increased from 5 to 33 percent between 1965 and 1975. And many professional schools previously closed to women have recently begun to admit female students. [13]

Despite some improvements, particularly at the professional level, women workers remain concentrated in stereotyped jobs with low pay, low status, and little opportunity for advancement. With this combination of disadvantages, why are more women working for pay, or seeking to do so? A combination of negative and positive factors, of compulsion and choice, are operating to weaken the more traditional division of labor, under which men have primary res-ponsibility for earning money while women's labor is mainly devoted to producing goods and services for home consumption.

One important element among the negative factors forcing women into the work force is the disintegration of families as a result of deepening poverty. In a country such as Bangladesh, which presents perhaps the clearest example of this phenomenon, the extended household is the ideal family structure. The women of the extended family work in seclusion within the family compound to service and maintain the household, while the men work the fields or pursue some other occupation in the public world outside. This ideal is so strongly held that women are allowed very few opportunities for formal employment. Unfortunately for Bengali women, the ideal and the economic reality are increasingly at variance. Joint families, which in theory can be relied upon to care for their weak or disinherited members, can actually be maintained only by the economically secure. The strain on agricultural resources relative to population in Ban-gladesh has produced a strong trend toward nuclear or even frac-tional households. Few families can afford to support a widowed daughter, sister, or sister-in-law. In a Bengali village studied by Mead Cain of the Population Council, for example, only 15 percent of the households were joint ones, and nearly one-third of the village's widows were engaged in a grim struggle for existence as wage-earning, "independent" heads of households.[14]

The situation in Bangladesh illustrates several of the negative pressures that are forcing increasing numbers of women to work for pay. Increasing poverty is the most obvious of these, not only because it contributes to family disintegration, but also because poverty makes it more difficult for traditional families to survive on men's earnings only. Additional pressure is associated with the growing number of households in which women are the only breadwinners—a trend fueled not only by poverty but by migration, by rising divorce rates, and sometimes by conscious choice. The insecurity of dependent status is daily illustrated to women in many parts of the world, wherever they live their lives only a man's heartbeat away from destitution.

In both rich countries and poor, inflation encourages women to work for pay. This mechanism has a psychological as well as an economic element, for inflation does not always generate poverty. Even if real income rises along with prices, the need for a higher money income produces a perceived need to spread the family's risks and to build up some protection against a possible real decline in buying power. Of course, when prices do outstrip gains in real income, as they did in Britain in the mid-seventies, many families can maintain a given standard of living only by relying on two income earners.

Two concomitants of modernization increase pressure on women to earn an income: progressive monetization of the economy and urbanization. Machine-made goods and goods that are not locally produced quickly find a place even in subsistence economies and assume the status of necessities. Kerosene, salt, sugar, tea, coffee, tobacco, agricultural inputs such as fertilizers and pesticides, machine-made cloth, and innumerable other items add to a household's need for cash. Previously unavailable services have the same effect, the most important of which are medical care and education. The desire to equip their children for a better life by providing cash for school fees, books, and supplies seems to be one of the most powerful motivations for women to try to earn money.

Urbanization cuts women off from the means of production available to rural dwellers. In the urban setting, women are often unable to gather fuel, grow crops, or forage for other necessities in the surrounding countryside. At the same time, new needs associated with city life present themselves: transportation costs, utility charges, rent payments, and so forth. Both the need to purchase goods and services that they could produce themselves in a rural setting and the cash requirements particular to city life help explain why more urban than rural women work for pay. Equally important is the urban woman's superior access to wage employment. Most developing countries are experiencing extremely rapid urbanization, a trend that guarantees that more women will enter the formal labor market.

In addition to these economic needs and pressures, there are some positive reasons women are joining the paid labor force. The ability to plan the number and the spacing of their children has freed many women from important constraints on their careers. Better preparation for employment, higher personal aspirations, and expanded opportunities have played parts in attracting women workers to paid employment.

In the developed countries, and some of the less developed nations, birth rates have fallen and life expectancy has risen dramatically in this century. Most women in these countries complete childbearing at an early age, and see their children go off to school while the mother is still quite young. As a result, for long stretches of adult life women are free of responsibility for full-time supervision of small children. The average Japanese woman, for example, has 42 years of life ahead of her after her youngest child goes to school. Many women in this position choose to enter or return to paid employment, or, increasingly, to combine the few years of preschool care with continuous employment.[15]

In most countries, there is a positive correlation between women's educational levels and their participation in the formal work force. In the United States, fewer than one out of four women with only an elementary-school education or less are in the labor force, compared with more than two out of three college graduates. Even in countries such as Egypt, Syria, and Turkey, where formal employment rates for women are below 10 percent, two out of three female college graduates work for pay. The positive correlation between education and paid employment also operates at lower levels of schooling, though it shows up most strongly if education extends at least through the secondary level. The link operates in two ways: educated women are more strongly motivated to work, and their training enables them to qualify for more-rewarding jobs. Steady progress in the numbers of girls and women who have access to formal education helps to explain why more women are working for pay.[16]

The most important of the positive factors drawing women into paid employment in recent years has been, unquestionably, the strong demand for their labor in the marketplace. In Western Europe, the United States, and Japan, this demand for women workers was the product of a sustained period of high growth in the sixties and early seventies, led by the expansion of the service sector of the economy. In China, it was the result of a conscious policy decision made in the context of a strenuous, labor-intensive development effort. In Taiwan, Hong Kong, and South Korea, rapid industrialization relied on poorly paid female factory operatives to hone a competitive edge in export markets. In many countries, the demand for female labor has been backed up with guarantees of women's economic rights through anti-discrimination legislation, positive programs to advance women's employment, and special training opportunities.

A serious question for employed women is whether the gains recently made when demand for labor was strong can be sustained in times of slow growth or stagnation. In general, women do not fare well in recessions. They usually experience higher unemployment rates than men, and in a chronic employment squeeze may be edged out of the formal labor force altogether. Most studies show that the majority of

*"A serious question for employed women
is whether gains recently made
when demand for labor was strong
can be sustained in times
of slow growth or stagnation."*

"discouraged workers"—those who leave the labor force because
their search for work has been fruitless—are women.

19

Paradoxically, women seem to be partially protected from unemployment by the very force that holds back their general economic advancement: occupational segregation. Usually the first sector of an industrial economy to suffer in a recession is heavy industry, the sector that employs the fewest women. The impact on the service sector, in which most women work, tends to filter down slowly. If the recession is neither too deep nor too prolonged, the service sector may experience a relatively mild slowdown. In the early stages of the global recession in the mid-seventies, this pattern seemed to hold. It was of little help to women workers, however, as the recession deepened. Women's unemployment started out at a higher level than men's. And female unemployment, though it rose more slowly at first, remained at a higher level throughout the downturn and declined more slowly as the economy revived.[17]

Breaking out of occupational stereotypes is much more difficult in times of slow growth than in periods of prosperity. If the global economy is indeed entering a period of sustained crisis, it will require extraordinary determination on the part of women and unprecedented commitment from governments to keep women's access to paid employment from being eroded.

Unpaid Labor: Women's Work Still

The trend toward greater participation in paid labor on the part of women has not been matched by an increased involvement of men in unpaid work. The particular tasks involved in maintaining a home vary enormously according to the resources available to the household, the size of the family, and the access to modern conveniences and commercial services. The time spent in household labor, interestingly enough, seems to vary much less. Middle-class housewives in modern, well-serviced homes still put in the long hours of household labor characteristic of women in more primitive circumstances. A higher standard of household services is as important as higher income to a rising standard of living.

The household work of women in poor, rural communities is extremely arduous. It typically involves heavy physical labor with primitive manual tools. Food production is often a major component of women's work in rural settings, and food processing is almost always a major task. Mead Cain discovered, for example, that women in Bangladesh spend nearly 25 hours a week in rice processing and other food preparation. Ruth Dixon has pointed out that a woman in rural Pakistan spends more than 14 hours a day working to meet her family's basic needs.[18] (See Table 2.)

Table 2: Time Spent on Daily Domestic Activities by Women in a Pakistani Village

Activity	Time Spent	Proportion of Waking Time
	(hours)	(percent)
Care and Feeding of Livestock	5.50	35
Milking and Churning	1.00	7
Cooking	1.75	11
Carrying Food to Fields and Feeding Children	1.50	10
House Cleaning and Making Dung Cakes for Fuel	.75	5
Carrying Water	.50	3
Child Care	.50	3
Other Domestic Chores (inc. food processing, crafts)	3.00	19
Afternoon Rest	1.00	7
Total Waking Hours	15.50	

Source: Ruth Dixon.

The importance of this kind of daily labor is underscored by the findings of an ILO study in Upper Volta. ILO staff workers there observed that family nutrition deteriorated during the rainy season, when nutritional needs were highest, because the adult women were too exhausted from agricultural work to cook. The major constraint on adequate nutrition at this time of year was not the food supply but the supply of female labor.[19]

The classic economic formulation of the relation between income and leisure predicts that the two rise in concert. For women in rural households, the opposite often seems to be the case. Higher household income typically means that there will be more food to process, more children and other relatives to supervise and to cook for, more wood and water to be provided, a larger house and compound to be maintained, more livestock to tend. Higher-income households are more likely to hire people to help with men's work in the fields or in businesses than they are to pay for someone to help women in the fields or around the house.

Most women in more-developed economies have been relieved of the heavy labor involved in basic household provisioning (water, food, fuel) and food processing. Technology has lightened the physical burden of housework in the modern home, yet it has not reduced the time comparable groups of women spend on domestic work by very much. Many observers have expressed astonishment at this fact. With washing machines, electric stoves, vacuum cleaners, and other appliances to improve their productivity, why do women still work such long hours—50 or more per week—in the household?

The question itself is revealing. It betrays a view of women's unpaid labor in the home as undifferentiated and unproductive above a certain minimum level. It is not the sort of question that is likely to be asked about a person who works for pay. No one would ask physicians or lawyers making $50 per hour why they continue to work 40 hours a week or more, despite the fact that their families' basic needs could be met with the income from a greatly reduced work schedule. Women work long and hard within the home for the same reason that they, and men, work long and hard outside it: to raise their own and their family's standard of living.

The University of Michigan has undertaken a large-scale, long-term survey of the use of time in American households. Between 1965 and 1975 there was a slight downward drift in the amount of time women spent in "family care," a category that includes housework, child care, transportation of family members, shopping, and other tasks usually done without pay for a household. The survey showed that comparable groups of women spent an average of two and one-half hours per week less on family care in 1975 than in 1965—an average of 22 minutes per day.[20]

In examining the survey data for information on the effect of household technology on women's work load, one scholar found that, contrary to expectations, technology had no effect on time spent on housework. Noting that ownership of appliances was positively correlated with income, he concluded that his findings "may mean that higher-income women simply have or set more ambitious goals for what housework can be accomplished in the time available."[21]

The two-and-one-half-hour decline in women's weekly household work load over the decade was found to be associated with demographic changes rather than with revisions in women's methods, routines, or accomplishments. The most important changes were in marital status, family size, and paid employment. On the average, women in 1975 were more likely to be unmarried, to work for pay, and to have fewer children than women in 1965. The decline in women's work was not compensated for by increased work by other family members.[22]

Sociologist Joann Vanek has observed that "the allocation of work in the home continues to be shaped by deeply ingrained ideas about the role of the sexes." In no area are these ideas more deeply ingrained than in the area of child care. The firm identification of infant and child care as women's work is no doubt based on the biological role of the nursing mother—but it extends far beyond the breastfeeding stage. The responsibility is not a light one. The world child-woman ratio, a statistic that gives the number of children under five years of age for every 1,000 women aged 15 to 49, is estimated at 552 in 1980. On a worldwide basis, therefore, every other woman in her prime productive years has a toddler to care for.[23]

Children under five are not, of course, distributed evenly around the world. There are marked regional variations in the child-woman ratio, with much higher ratios prevailing in the Third World than in the industrial countries. In North Africa and the Middle East, for example, there are roughly 800 children under five for every 1,000 women aged 15 to 49, whereas in Europe and North America the figure is less than half that. However, the requirements of child care vary with culture and circumstances in ways that belie any direct extrapolation of the child-care work load from the number of children present. In North Yemen, for example, where nearly half the population is under 15, Carla Makhlouf reports that child care occupies very little of women's time: "Child rearing patterns are very permissive; children are not given a great deal of surveillance and are left to play with neighbor's children."[24] In a village or neighborhood setting that is perceived as safe for children, younger ones may be left in the care of only slightly older ones, thus relieving mothers of their supervisory tasks.

Time-budget studies show that child care occupies little of rural women's time, usually 10 percent or less. The reason may be that the supervision of children is not seen as a separate activity. It occupies the same time and space as do other tasks. Also, poor women may find their time so thoroughly occupied with meeting the basic physical needs of the family that child care as a distinct activity is an unaffordable luxury. Such was the conclusion of a comprehensive government report on the status of women in India, issued in 1975: "Women of the poorer sections whose days are spent in hard labor (in earning and housework) are extremely overworked and can give little attention to the bringing up of children."[25]

In assessing the effect of children on women's total work load it must be remembered that children can shoulder some of the responsibility for household maintenance, starting at quite an early age to lighten their mothers' work loads to some extent. An ILO report on the condition of rural women in Zaire cites a survey in one province, which showed that girls aged 10 to 14 carried a work load equal to 55 percent of a full-grown woman's—this in a setting in which adult men do only one-third as much work as adult women. Even little girls, aged five to nine, did 5 percent of an adult woman's work. Boys in that age-group made no contribution to the household labor, while 10-to-14-year-old boys did 15 percent as much as their mothers. So the effect of children, especially of daughters, for rural Zairian women probably is a net reduction of work time.[26]

The impact of children is very different in a setting where formal workplaces are physically separated from the home and are age-segregated. Child care acquires a concrete opportunity cost when it becomes incompatible with other kinds of work, when women must choose whether to stay with their children or go out to work. The net gain of going to work is lowered when a family must find a replacement for a parent's presence with the children. Because child care is so firmly identified as a female responsibility, the costs associated with it are attributed to women almost exclusively. Dr. James Levine of Wellesley College points out that even the most progressive governments still confront child care in terms of *women's* changing roles. Changes in the number of children with working mothers are monitored carefully, but statistics on children of working fathers are not even compiled.[27]

Carrying the major responsibility for child care and other unpaid labor handicaps women in the formal labor market. The second shift at home competes with the demands of the workplace for women's time, energy, and attention. The handicap becomes especially acute for women who aspire to leadership positions, for such achievement usually demands more than a routine workday. Extra hours on the job, union activism, political involvement, adult education, volunteer work, civic or cultural leadership—all common prerequisites for outstanding performance—amount in themselves to a second shift. Employed women with families who pursue such positions end up

"The second shift at home competes
with the demands of the workplace
for women's time, energy,
and attention."

working a triple day. As long as private lives and public institutions are arranged around the assumption that the home is a female **25** province, women's opportunities for achievement in other domains will be limited.

The Division of Labor Between Women and Men

As more women around the world have started working for pay, out of choice or necessity, the traditional division of labor has lost its definition. Men no longer monopolize gainful employment outside the home, even in theory. But while this change has become firmly established, women have retained an unwilling monopoly on unpaid labor within the household. Only one side of the ancient division has broken down. The result is a pronounced imbalance in male and female work loads, with unhappy consequences for women, men, and children.

There are several explanations for the prevailing asymmetry between men's and women's work. One of the most fundamental hinges on the difference in pay and prestige attached to masculine and feminine tasks as conventionally defined. Typically, men's work is more richly rewarded than women's, both in money and status. So it is no wonder that women seek access to it. The only element of women's economic role that commands such high social rewards as to be enviable is one that is biologically foreclosed to men—childbearing. Most of women's work is so poorly paid (if paid at all) and poorly regarded that men have seldom tried to make inroads into it. Women have tried with some success to break into the ranks of corporate executives, for example, yet few men have sought admission to the ranks of file clerks. Similarly—and with more serious consequences for the division of labor—women have campaigned for equality in the labor force and public life, but men have not made an issue of equal access to housework and home life.

Another reason for the growing imbalance between the amount of work done by men and women is the different susceptibility of each sphere to the manipulations of public policy. Men's paid labor takes place mostly in the public domain, whereas women's unpaid labor tends to be confined to the household economy. This has affected the division of labor in two ways. First, men's work has been altered by official decision making and in many instances their work load has been lightened. Legislation on wages and hours, for example, has steadily reduced the amount of work time required to earn a living. The standard paid workweek in industrial countries is now 40 to 45 hours, down from 60 or so earlier in this century. Women's work, however, has been regarded as belonging strictly to the private sphere, where governmental reforms and regulations have no place.

Second, the public nature of the masculine sphere of work has meant the state could forcibly alter the access of women to formal employment with equal-opportunity legislation, penalties for discrimination, and so forth. But the state has no such leverage over the division of labor in the household, the feminine sphere. A few governments—China, Cuba, and Sweden being the most prominent examples—have made the sharing of housework a tenet of official policy. But all three recognize that official endorsement of the idea is a rhetorical device and that the policy is impossible to enforce in practical terms.[28] Government's power to shift the overall division of labor (encompassing both market and nonmarket work) between men and women is lopsided. It is much more capable of increasing women's market work than of decreasing their nonmarket labor, and more capable of decreasing men's paid labor than of increasing their unpaid work at home.

The unequal division of labor is not the problem of a small minority. In most industrial countries, married women have been the fastest-growing segment of the paid labor force in the postwar period. In Britain, the United States, Canada, Sweden, and the East European countries, more than half the female labor force is currently made up of married women.[29] Moreover, there has been a substantial increase in the number of working wives who are also mothers, even mothers of young children. This represents a major shift in the pattern of women's employment outside the home.

"Families in which both husband
and wife work outside the home
have become the most common
pattern in the United States."

In the early stages of industrialization, the wage-earning female
labor force was composed mainly of single women, for whom family
responsibilities were minimal. This pattern still prevails in the new
industrial states of Southeast Asia and in Latin America, where labor
force participation rates are highest among women in their teens and
early twenties.[30] In later stages of industrialization, women's employment rates often exhibit two peaks, one in the early years before
childbearing and one after children have gone to school or, later, have
become self-sufficient. The two peaks of labor-market activity strad-
dle the period of life when domestic responsibilities are at their
heaviest.

During the seventies, a new pattern of uninterrupted paid employment for married women with children flattened the two peaks in
female labor-market activity in many industrial countries. Women
in the younger age groups in particular showed an increasing ten-
dency to combine paid work with childbearing and domestic responsibilities. The number of working mothers in the United States rose
ninefold between 1945 and 1975, with the result that families in
which both husband and wife work outside the home have become
the most common pattern in the United States.[31]

Survey after survey has examined the way men and women spend
their time, and the findings on working women's disproportionate
share of the total work load are remarkably uniform, whether one
examines developed or developing countries, capitalist or socialist
economies, agricultural or industrial societies. The United Nations'
review of progress for women in the first half of the UN Decade for
Women (1975-85), based on information submitted by 86 member
governments, noted bluntly that "in all cases studied the amount
of leisure time of employed women was less than that of employed
men." Though women who work for pay spend less time at paid
jobs, on the average, than men do as well as less time at household labors than nonemployed women, the total number of hours
they spend working surpasses the total of either men or nonemployed
women—often by as much as 10 to 15 hours a week.[32] (See Table 3.)

Table 3: Average Time-Budget of Employed Men, Employed Women, and Housewives in 12 Countries, 1975*

Daily Activities	Employed Men		Employed Women		Housewives	
	Workday	Day Off	Workday	Day Off	Weekday	Sunday
	(hours)					
Total Work	10.6	3.5	11.6	6.1	8.9	6.0
Paid Work	9.4	.9	7.9	.4	.2	.1
Housework	1.0	2.3	3.3	5.1	7.6	5.2
Child Care	.2	.3	.4	.6	1.1	.7
Sleep, Meals, Personal Needs	9.9	12.2	9.9	11.9	11.1	11.7
Free Time	3.5	8.3	2.5	6.0	4.0	6.3
Total	24.0	24.0	24.0	24.0	24.0	24.0
Total Workweek**	60		70.2		56.5	
Total Free Time Per Week**	34		14.5		32.6	

*Belgium, Bulgaria, Czechoslovakia, France, Federal Republic of Germany, German Democratic Republic, Hungary, Peru, Poland, United States, USSR, and Yugoslavia. The survey did not cover purely agricultural households where members worked only on farms.
**Assumes five working days and two days off.
Source: Adapted from Alexander Szalai.

Along with the entry of married women to the labor force, another contributor to the skewing of the sexual division of labor is the increased number of women who head families on their own. Women who are sole heads of households usually have full responsibility for both income-earning and household labor, including the care and support of children. Because of a rise in divorce, increased numbers of widows, the migration of men and women at different rates, and childbearing outside of any stable union with a man, women-headed households represent a substantial minority in many countries. Such households make up 14 percent of American and 17 percent of Russian families. One-fourth of Venezuelan households are headed by women alone, as are one-third in some Caribbean countries. In parts of Kenya the proportion reaches 40 percent.[33]

For mothers who become heads of households through divorce or abandonment, financial support from the fathers of their children is rare. In the United States, mothers are awarded custody in nine out of ten divorces that involve children, but only 44 percent of them are awarded child support—and two-thirds of these women have so much trouble collecting the awarded payments that they eventually seek legal redress.[34] Financial support is a serious problem for widows, too, especially in countries where inheritance laws favor male kinsmen over the wife of a deceased man. To an even greater extent than married women who work outside the home, women who head households have a double burden of responsibility.

For families in which both an adult man and an adult woman work for pay, solutions to the problem of the woman's double day fall into three basic categories: delegating part of the household responsibilities to people or institutions outside the family, reducing the size of the household's overall work load, or sharing the total work load more equitably among family members. These alternatives can be pursued singly or in combination, and people select different hybrids to suit their own circumstances.

The delegation of some household reponsibilities to people outside the family has been both a cause and an effect of the postwar growth of the service sector. With modernization, some of the tasks previously performed by the women of the household move into the marketplace. Bread baking, fuel and water provision, clothes making, and other similar services are progressively taken over by commercial enterprises. The expansion of the service sector often creates a strong demand for female labor, thus reinforcing the need for additional services to replace the household labor of the newly employed women.

This process of substitution continues at all levels of modernization. With more women working for pay, not only does the demand for replacement services grow, but the higher incomes of two-earner families make the purchase of a wider range of services possible. A typical American family, for example, now spends one-fourth of its food budget on meals eaten away from home—a phenomenon that is widely attributed to the rising number of working women.[35]

Substitution for housewives' services has been pushed vigorously by some governments as a way of raising the overall productivity of the population, of bringing women into the work force to make up for a shortfall of labor, or of promoting equal status for women and men. All three objectives are explicit in the theoretical underpinnings of communist societies. In 1884, Frederick Engels argued in *The Origin of the Family, Private Property and the State* that "the emancipation of women becomes possible only when women are enabled to take part in production on a large, social scale, and when domestic duties require their attention only to a minor degree." Engels predicted that with the establishment of Communism, "private housekeeping is transformed into a social industry. The care and education of the children becomes a public matter."[36]

The reality of housework and child care in Eastern Europe, the Soviet Union, and other communist countries is a far cry from the ideal state pictured by Engels. Actual provision of services by the state is patchy, and in many cases unsatisfactory, despite the fact that female labor force participation rates there are the world's highest. Women in communist countries, like wage-earning women everywhere, still work a double day. According to one estimate, the average Russian woman spends three to four hours a day on housework after working a full day at a paying job.[37]

Where the delegation of household responsiblities either to the state or to commercial providers of services is not yet a practical alternative, women respond to the rigors of the double day by trying to reduce their total work loads. One of the most popular means is part-time employment. Many women limit the time they spend in paid employment so that they can meet their domestic obligations. In early 1980, approximately 29 percent of American women in paid

"The average Russian woman
spends three to four hours a day
on housework after working
a full day at a paying job."

employment worked part-time (less than 35 hours per week). This proportion is not very much higher than that of men. But women's part-time work is concentrated in their childbearing years, whereas men are more likely to work part-time at the beginning or end of working life.[38]

Another method of reducing the total work load is to cut down household labor requirements. The amount of work done in the home can simply be reduced, an approach that is difficult to evaluate. If less time is spent cleaning house, preparing food, supervising children, mending clothing or housewares, the result may be a real decline in the family's standard of living. This is a particular danger for poor, rural households, where women's household labor is responsible for meeting so many of their families' basic needs. On the other hand, some households may tolerate a reduced level of non-market services without any sense of deprivation at all.

A second, and more definitive, way to reduce household responsibilities is to have smaller families. This response has become epidemic in Eastern Europe, to the great consternation of governments that are worried about the size of the future labor force. Only 18 percent of Soviet families, for example, had five or more members in 1979, and 59 percent consisted of three persons or fewer.[39] The one-child family has become commonplace throughout Eastern Europe. Most of the countries in the region have instituted generous leave and allowance policies for mothers, but in most the birth rate has failed to rise. Only recently has it been suggested that one way to solve the problem of women's overwork is for men to do some of the work around the home, at least until Engel's dream of socialized housework materializes.

The Chinese Government, by contrast, encourages smaller families, and has been quick to point out that fewer children means a lighter work load for women. The government is pushing the idea of the two-child family as a maximum, and even advocates strongly that couples stop at one. The main reason for this policy is the staggering size of the country's population and its threatening potential for

31

growth, but the effect on women's emancipation has not been overlooked.[40]

Perhaps the most obvious way to reduce the employed woman's dual
burden of paid and unpaid labor is for men to do a greater share of
the housework and child care. Cuba wrote this obligation into its new
family code, promulgated in 1975. In China, the government has
acknowledged, speaking through the leading theoretical journal in
that country, that it "is necessary to advocate that men and women
should share household chores." In these, as in most other countries,
the theory has been easier to establish than the practice. Although
housewives who depend solely on a husband's income are now rare
in China, women still have primary responsibility for cooking,
housework, and child care. Furthermore, women do not receive any
work points for these activities. As a result, they receive a smaller
share of communal earnings.[41]

It is easy to scoff at official exhortations for men to do more work
at home, but the effect of such policies over time may outweigh their
often negligible short-term impact. One of the reasons that has been
identified for men's reluctance to increase their responsibility in the
household is a strong set of social disincentives to do so. A survey
of dual-career families in the United States found that, even in families where both spouses worked for pay, men could expect teasing
or scorn from their peers if they spent an unusual amount of time on
housework or child care.[42] To the extent that official stances can
help to break down such attitudes, they may encourage a more
equitable division of labor. Many governments, however, especially in
the industrial West, regard the division of labor within the family as
none of their business.

The Symmetrical Family

Progress toward a new, egalitarian division of labor in the world of
paid employment is undercut by the persistence of the old, unequal

division of domestic labor. Sociologist Rita Liljestrom has suggested that today's working woman is caught in a time lag between two **33** waves of social change: the first swept away the acceptability of discrimination in formal employment; the second will dissolve discrimination on the home front. Hers is a hopeful formulation, for it endows the succession of events with an inevitability that many overworked women now have cause to doubt.[43]

Part of their doubt stems from a deep ambivalence on the part of governments toward the role of women in society, which is both derived from and reflected in widespread individual ambivalence. The principle that women should be free to work outside the home—and should be free of discrimination when they do—is accepted by most governments. But the idea that women are the guardians of the home and the primary nurturers of children is deeply ingrained in family laws and labor codes throughout the world.

Employers are bound to give women short shrift if they can assume correctly that women will normally be the parents to leave their jobs, even if only temporarily, to care for young children; that they will be the ones to take time off when children fall sick; that they will refuse overtime work because of household responsibilities; that they will relocate when their spouses are transferred to other jobs. These assumptions inevitably prejudice women's standing in the labor force. Governments aggravate the problem when they attempt to make it easier for women to fit the assumptions rather than making it easier for men and women to share family responsibilities.

There is a double standard for women workers: it asserts that their conditions of work should permit them to fulfill all the obligations of their traditional role while taking on a whole new set of obligations associated with formal employment. It also stoutly maintains that women should not be forced to work outside the home—a bit of wishful thinking that is manifestly unfair to women who must work to support themselves. The double standard is also unfair to men, who are never offered the choice—however fanciful—of not working outside the home.

A 1975 memorandum on equal treatment for male and female workers issued by the European Commission for its nine member governments illustrates the prevalent official ambivalence toward women's roles. On the one hand it embraced the objective of ending the "all too frequent disequilibrium in employment, promotion opportunities and working conditions"; on the other, it recommended "the introduction of more flexible hours to allow for female workers' family responsibilities."[44]

A number of measures commonly offered as solutions to the problems of women's dual role actually reinforce the traditional division of labor. Increased availability of part-time work and flexible hours are commonly presented as aids to working women. Similarly, child care is almost always presented as a "woman's issue." Both, when seen as benefits for women, reinforce the assumption that women carry the major responsibility for home and children and that their economic roles are secondary.

Attempts to solve the conflict between workplace and family that focus exclusively on women's roles entrench discrimination against women in the labor force. Many countries have labor laws that are meant to protect women from overwork and preserve their ability to meet family responsibilities. East Germany, for example, gives working mothers one day of paid leave per month so that they can attend to housework and child care; women with several children are entitled to shorter working hours and longer holidays with no reduction in pay.[45] There is no question that women benefit from measures of this kind in the short run, but the benefits are a poor substitute for genuine equality in work and family life. The long-term effect is to freeze women in secondary jobs, for employers will continue to prefer workers who can measure up to a full-time standard.

In a tight labor market, special provisions for women workers may undercut their ability to compete for jobs on an equal footing with men. David Chaplin has documented the sharp drop in female industrial employment in Peru that occurred when special benefits for women workers were introduced in 1959. He found that some textile

"A number of measures
commonly offered as solutions to
the problems of women's dual role
actually reinfore the traditional
division of labor."

factories did not hire any new female workers after the new benefits were introduced entitling women to 72 days of maternity leave at 70 percent salary. The reforms also limited women's workweek to 45 hours but obliged employers to pay women for the standard 48-hour week. As a result, women became more expensive to hire than men, and many employers virtually stopped hiring them.[46]

The negative impact of the Peruvian reforms could have been at least partially overcome by transferring the cost of the benefits from individual employers to the social welfare system, so that employers would not have had such a strong incentive to stop hiring women workers. The discriminatory effect could have been further reduced if leave had been available equally to fathers and mothers, and if the reduction of the workweek to allow for family responsibilities had been applied regardless of sex.

The reconciliation of work and family responsibilities is not just a woman's issue. But very few governments have begun to address this question in a way that would enable men and women to participate equally in both employment and family life. Of those that have, Sweden's is probably the most comprehensive program. The tax system adopted by the Swedish Government in 1970 considers the personal incomes of all adults without reference to family status. Previously a husband and wife were taxed together, and the higher tax payments of the two-income family effectively devalued the wife's earnings. The reforms also made the income tax more steeply progressive, so that two incomes have become more and more of a necessity for the average family.[47]

In 1974, parenthood insurance, one of the most progressive elements of Swedish family policy, was introduced. The insurance allows parents nine months' leave upon the birth of a child, to be apportioned between the mother and father as they see fit. While receiving 90 percent of their regular salary, either parent can choose to stay away from work for one long period or several short ones. Alternatively, the leave can be prorated so that parents can shorten their workdays to half- or three-quarter-time while the child is young. Parents not gainfully employed at the time of a birth are entitled to an allowance in lieu of salary. Up to ten additional days of leave per year are available if the mother or father needs to stay home to care for a sick child. A 1979 revision of the system gives parents of children under the age of eight the right to work a six-hour day, though in this case the reduced time is not compensated.[48]

The tax and insurance measures in Sweden are components of a general policy to encourage and facilitate greater involvement of women in the labor force and greater involvement of men in family life. Other important elements of the strategy include an expansion of public child care and educational facilities (though these are still unable to accommodate all eligible children), a conscious effort to break down occupational segregation, and a steady reduction of salary differentials between male and female workers.[49] All of these measures operate in the context of a strong full-employment policy.

The results of the Swedish experiment have been equivocal. The number of women leaving the labor force after having children went down markedly during the seventies—only 13 percent of working women who had first children between 1975 and 1977 stopped working outside the home, compared with 29 percent from 1970 to 1972. But the number of men who took advantage of the parental insurance grew very slowly. Currently only 10 to 12 percent of fathers take time off from work to look after their children. A more traditional solution to the double day is still common in Sweden: 45 percent of the employed women work part-time in order to cope with family responsibilities.[50]

Although Sweden has made the most far-reaching effort to reconcile family policy with employment policy and to encourage the development of the symmetrical family, other governments have implemented measures compatible with these goals. France and East Germany, for example, have set up nearly universal systems of pre-school care for children over three years of age, as well as substantial facilities for the care of younger children. France and Norway both allow fathers as well as mothers to take leave upon the birth or illness of a child.[51]

Clearly, the division of labor within a private household can be influenced by public policy only up to a certain point. It remains a privately determined matter, a subject for communication and negotiation between the man and woman directly involved. The role of the state is important, but limited. It must try to ensure that people have adequate resources to provide for their own needs and those of their dependents; it must acknowledge the social and economic contributions of all productive people without prejudice; and it must set the framework for equality between the sexes by removing all obstacles to equal opportunity in the labor force and the household. The latter requires broadened definitions of men's as well as women's roles. The assumption that women are superior parents is no more justified than is the assumption that men are superior breadwinners.

Perhaps the most effective thing a government can do to encourage equality in private life is to enforce equality in the public sphere of paid employment. Studies from many different countries show that the women who enjoy the greatest equality in their personal relationships with men are those who are closest to their mates in education, occupational prestige, and earnings. If women continue to be cast in secondary roles in the labor force, it will seem natural for them to shoulder most of the responsibility at home. Women's longer hours of housework are often viewed by both them and their mates as justifiable compensation for their smaller financial contributions to the family. If this economic obstacle to equality can be removed, other seemingly immovable cultural obstacles may, over time, yield with surprising grace.

1. Michael Young and Peter Willmott, *The Symmetrical Family* (London: Routledge & Kegan Paul, 1975), cited in Rita Liljeström, "Integration of Family Policy and Labour Market Policy in Sweden," *Social Change in Sweden*, December 1978.

39

2. Derek W. Blades, *Non-Monetary (Subsistence) Activities in the National Accounts of Developing Countries* (Paris: Organisation for Economic Cooperation and Development, 1975).

3. M. Dean, quoted in Blades, *Non-Monetary Activities.*

4. Blades, *Non-Monetary Activities.*

5. David A. Mitchnik, *The Role of Women in Rural Zaire and Upper Volta: Improving Methods of Skill Acquisition* (Geneva: International Labour Office, 1976).

6. International Labour Office (ILO), *La Participation des Femmes a l'Activité Economique dans le Monde (Analyse Statistique)* (Geneva: March 1980).

7. 1950 figures from Population Reference Bureau, *Interchange*, March 1977; 1980 figures from Bureau of Labor Statistics, *Employment in Perspective: Working Women*, U.S. Department of Labor, Washington, D.C., No. 4, 1979.

8. "Report of the Secretary-General," Commission on the Status of Women of the United Nations Economic and Social Council, 28th Session, Vienna, February 25-March 5, 1980.

9. Linda Y. C. Lim, "Women Workers in Multinational Companies in Developing Countries," in *Women and Development*, prepared by Irene Tinker (Washington, D.C.: American Association for the Advancement of Science, 1979).

10. Figure for Latin America as a whole from ILO, *Participation des Femmes;* specific country figures from International Labour Office, *Conditions of Work, Vocational Training and Employment of Women*, 11th Congress of American States (Geneva: 1979).

11. "Report of the Secretary-General."

12. *Ibid.*

13. Kathleen Newland, *The Sisterhood of Man* (New York: W. W. Norton & Co., 1979).

14. Mead Cain, Syeda Rokeya Khanam, and Shamsum Nahar, "Class, Patriarchy, and the Structure of Women's Work in Rural Bangladesh," Working Paper No. 43, Population Council, New York, May 1979.

15. Merry White, "Women in Japan, the Public and Private Spheres: A Theoretical Overview," presented to a meeting of the Association for Asian Studies, Chicago, Illinois, March 31-April 2, 1978.

16. "One in Three Workers Has Gone to College," Bureau of Labor Statistics, U.S. Department of Labor, Washington, D.C., February 14, 1980; Newland, *The Sisterhood of Man.*

17. *ILO Information*, Vol. 4, No. 6, 1976.

18. Cain, Khanam, and Nahar, "Class, Patriarchy, and the Structure of Women's Work in Rural Bangladesh"; Ruth B. Dixon, *Rural Women at Work* (Baltimore: Johns Hopkins University Press for Resources for the Future, 1978).

19. Mitchnik, *The Role of Women in Rural Zaire and Upper Volta.*

20. John P. Robinson, "Housework Technology and Household Work," in Sarah Fernstermaker Berk, ed., *Women and Household Labor* (Beverly Hills: Sage Publications, 1980).

21. *Ibid.*

22. *Ibid.*

23. Joann Vanek, "Household Work, Wage Work, and Sexual Equality," in Berk, *Women and Household Labor;* the global child-woman ratio is an estimate by the author based on Population Division, "World Population and Its Age-Sex Composition by Country, 1950-2000: Demographic Estimation and Projection as Assessed in 1978," United Nations, New York, January 2, 1980.

24. Regional child-woman ratio are estimates by the author based on Population Division, "World Population and Its Age-Sex Composition"; Carla Makhlouf, *Changing Veils: Women and Modernization in North Yemen* (Austin, Texas: University of Texas Press, 1979).

25. Indian Council of Social Science Research, *Status of Women in India: A Synopsis of the Report of the National Committee of the Status of Women* (New Delhi: 1975).

26. Mitchnik, *The Role of Women in Rural Zaire and Upper Volta.*

27. James A. Levine, "Redefining the Child Care 'Problem'—Men as Child Nurturers," *Childhood Education,* November/December 1977.

28. Newland, *The Sisterhood of Man.*

29. International Labour Office, *Equal Opportunities and Equal Treatment for Men and Women Workers: Workers with Family Responsibilities,* International Labour Conference, 66th Session, 1980 (Geneva: 1979).

30. Newland, *The Sisterhood of Man.*

31. ILO, *Equal Opportunities and Equal Treatment.*

32. "Report of the Secretary-General"; Alexander Szalai, "The Situation of Women in the Light of Contemporary Time-Budget Research," U.N. World Conference of International Women's Year, Mexico City, June 19-July 2, 1975.

42

33. Bureau of Labor Statistics, *Employment in Perspective: Working Women,* U.S. Department of Labor, Washington, D.C., 1979 Summary; Bernice Madison, "Soviet Women: The 'Problemy' That Won't Go Away," *Wilson Quarterly,* Autumn 1978; Mayra Buvinić and Nadia H. Youssef, *Women-Headed Households: The Ignored Factor in Development Planning* (Washington, D.C.: International Center for Research on Women, 1978).

34. Newland, *The Sisterhood of Man.*

35. Walter Kiechel III, "Two Income Families Will Reshape the Consumer Markets," *Fortune,* March 10, 1980.

36. Frederick Engels quoted in Hilda Scott, *Does Socialism Liberate Women?* (Boston: Beacon Press, 1974).

37. Madison, "Soviet Women."

38. Bureau of Labor Statistics, *Employment in Perspective: Working Women,* U.S. Department of Labor, Washington, D.C., No. 1, 1980.

39. Gennadi Gerasimov, "The Soviet Family: How Big?," *Soviet Life,* March 1980.

40. Elisabeth Croll, *Women in Rural Development: The People's Republic of China* (Geneva: International Labour Office, 1979).

41. "Chinese Men Are Told to Aid in Housework," *New York Times,* December 16, 1973; Croll, *Women in Rural Development.*

42. Laura Lein, "Male Participation in Home Life: Impact of Social Supports and Breadwinner Responsibility on the Allocation of Tasks," *Family Coordinator,* October 1979.

43. Liljeström, "Integration of Family Policy."

44. "Equal Opportunity for Working Women," *European File,* Commission of the European Communities, Brussels, April 1980.

45. "Report of the Secretary-General."

46. David Chaplin, *The Peruvian Industrial Labor Force* (Princeton, N.J.: Princeton University Press, 1967).

47. Liljeström, "Integration of Family Policy."

48. *Ibid;* "Europe's Innovative Family Policies," *Transatlantic Perspectives*, March 1980.

49. Elisabet Sandberg, *Equality Is The Goal* (Stockholm: Swedish Institute, 1975).

50. Siv Gustafsson, "Women and Work in Sweden," *Working Life in Sweden*, December 1979.

51. "Europe's Innovative Family Policies."

KATHLEEN NEWLAND is a Senior Researcher with Worldwatch Institute and author of *The Sisterhood of Man* (W. W. Norton, May 1979). Her research deals with human resources issues.

0680